POETRY AND STORIES
FOR PRIMARY AND LOWER
SECONDARY SCHOOLS

MICHAEL ROSEN

Introduction: Poetry and Literacy

Poetry for children can work as a bridge between the oral and the written. Its hooks of rhythm and pattern invite speaking and reading.

Make the connection for children: what can be spoken, can be written: voice, page: poems, jokes, stories, riddles, sayings, drama.

Every time a child likes hearing a poem (or part of one) make sure there is a written form of it available for them to revisit it as 'writing'.

Experimental sounds, experimental writing: loud-quiet, fast-slow, words-nonwords, exclamations, sound effects: voice, eye, ear. All this makes the connection between oral and written too.

Sing a song, read a song: voice, eye, page . . . hear a poem, read a poem: ear, eye, voice . . .

Adults say to me about writing (anything: reports, articles etc) they're stuck, I say 'Talk it, really or in your head, then write that.' Same thing works for children.

Literacy is not a quantity. It's a lived practice or behaviour. We want children to live in it and know it's theirs. One of the best ways to do this is to remind them again and again that what is said, can be written. Poetry is a great way to do that. Say it, read it, write it.

Part 1: The Starting Point

The starting point for poetry in primary schools must be poems. That's to say, not a worksheet, not a writing exercise but a pile of poems, a set of poems, a cornucopia of poems.

The first job is for the children to see that poems can become theirs, that poets wrote poems for the likes of them, that poems belong to them.

How can we best do that?

Poems have to become part of the classroom, part of school life and poems are things that children can browse and find for themselves; poems are things that are on walls, in books that are accessible at all times; poems can be heard, shouted, whispered, sung, given accompaniments with drawings, pictures on powerpoint, music, mime, film, whatever.

One simple place to start is to come in one day and say that in 20 minutes time we're going to have a poetry show. You distribute piles of poetry books on the children's tables. You invite the children to go into pairs and choose a poem per pair. You ask them to prepare a poem per pair for the poetry show that you're going to have in 20 minutes time. You tell them that they can perform the poem in anyway they like: taking turns, saying it together, singing some of it or all of it, tapping out a rhythm, miming it, making noises to go with it – leaving out words or lines for the rest of the class to guess . . . etc etc.

20 minutes later, you hold the poetry show. For this first one, you m.c.

3

the show making a big deal of it, making sure that everyone is ready and quite to hear each performance and giving each one applause.

At the end of the show of approx fifteen performances, you invite the children in their pairs to consider what aspects of each other's performances would they consider trying out for the next poetry show. This is a positive way to do criticism and builds the idea that you are a team trying to help each other get better and better at poetry together. If there was something you noticed that no one mentions you can chip in with. If there's something that you think might be worth trying e.g. making the sound of sea 'behind' a performance, you suggest that too.

A day later, or a two days later, or three days later or a week later you do the same again. Whatever interval you set up, you repeat, so there is an expectation for this activity to happen again and again. This is very important.

You keep this going for as long as there is enthusiasm.

You can vary the format by e.g. you and a child having a go. Involve the TAs. Widen the choice of poems. Let the children go back to favourites. Try using powerpoint, try making 'shoe boxes' to represent poems. Try doing paintings. If you're used to one of the animation apps, try that.

What is all this about?

This is not only about helping a class 'possess' poems, it is giving them a 'repertoire'. Each time you do the 'show', you might be covering 15 poems. You're building up many ways of how poems work. You're enabling the children to have poems in their minds, bodies and voices.

I can promise you that they will become enthusiastic about poetry because you're showing that you believe in poems and you believe in them. The point here is that poems are doing the work, and that's because poems have 'hooks'. Poets are people who write poems so that they 'stick' to readers and listeners: whether that's rhyme, rhythm, imagery, shape, repetition or whatever, each line of a poem holds within it the efforts of a poet to grab the attention of a reader or listener. These hooks are the most cogent argument for poetry – not commentary, not worksheets, but the poem itself.

Don't necessarily expect dramatic results immediately. Give it two or three sessions for the pattern to develop of performance/discussion/learning from each other/performance to take hold.

Alongside this, it's worth thinking about what else you can do to make a poetry-friendly classroom.

A bookshelf or bookcase of poetry books.

You could try writing out a poem a week on a huge bit of paper.

Invite the children to put post-its on and around the poem with comments and questions. On the day you're going to change the poem to a new one (a week later?) collect up the post-its and get the children to talk about them e.g. handing them out to pairs, followed by a plenary. If there are questions, discuss how best to answer them.

Watch or listen to poets performing their poems on CD, video, online or wherever.

Get poets to come to school.

Organise a poetry cabaret evening involving parents and grandparents.

Make sure that it only lasts about half an hour interspersed with music, dance and perhaps an art show.

Invite the children to make their own personal poetry anthologies. Give them each a nice notebook and tell them they can copy out any poem, part of a poem, song, part of a song, or any 'line' from something they hear on TV or on the radio that sounds interesting or caught their imagination – perhaps from a film. You do the same and show them your anthology and where you're collecting your poems and parts of poems and sayings from. This 'models' making an anthology.

These pages are all inter-connected. However your base is in reading poems together and sharing poems in a poetry-friendly classroom. It's here that poems do the 'work' for you. They will engender the enthusiasm and excitement you need.

Part 2: Why Poetry?

Some teachers have told me that on occasions people who manage schools have told them that they shouldn't just be letting children read to themselves, and/or they shouldn't just be reading and enjoying poetry. The teachers need to be doing some specific teaching and the children need to be doing a set task.

In this chapter, I'm going to try to answer this. I'm going to defend the activity of reading and enjoying poetry in the primary classroom. Just that. No task.

This involves me imagining a situation in which a teacher has to justify this in a meeting with someone who is telling that teacher that there is little or no point in simply reading and enjoying poetry.

Please feel free to adopt or adapt any of the following:

1. Learning to read is never simply or only a matter of decoding letters. No one says that it is. In order to learn how to understand words, phrases, paragraphs, verses, chapters and books, we have to relate what's on the page with 'meaning'. There are many ways of doing this. One way is to share the enjoyment of a piece of writing. One of the ways we can do this is to read, say, perform and talk about poems. In short, then, doing poems together in class is a great way of learning how writing has meaning. The shorthand for this is 'comprehension'. I prefer the word 'interpretation' because when any of us, children or adults, talk about something like a poem, we have different views of what things in the poem, or the poem as a whole means. We have different views on how we feel about the poem. We interpret parts and the whole of poem. The discussion we have around these different interpretations are great for discovering and refining ways in which words and phrases mean things.

So, poems are a great way of helping children learn to read for meaning.

2. Most poems are good for saying out loud, particularly ones that have been written for children, or ones for adults that have been selected specially for children. These kinds of poems, then, have a quality in them that is potentially oral: we can pass them to each other over the airwaves. This of course is what we do with speech. These poems are then a specialised form of speech. They have been written to be said. The importance for this with children is that it makes them ideal for being a kind of 'bridge' between the oral and the written.

Why might this be important?

I think we know that for some – possibly many children – the written word poses a challenge. Even when some of it makes sense, other parts of it don't. By having a written form that has feet in both the oral and the written word, poems enable children to move easily between the two. Poems they hear, they can then find on the page. Poems on the page can be turned into things that can be said.

What's more there are all sorts of hints and suggestions in poems about how to say them. And where there aren't, after a bit of reading two or three times, it's great to discover how reading poems out loud in different ways alters the meaning. In fact, every time a child engages with how to say a poem out loud, he or she actually engages with the meaning in a very easy and satisfying way.

So, again, for a slightly different reason, poems are great ways to help children read for meaning.

3. Real writing is never just words. As we all know, a test like the Phonics Screening Check is a list of words. That's because it is testing for children's ability to decode letters. Nearly all writing and reading outside of a test situation involves sequences of words (phrases, clauses, sentences, lines, verses, paragraphs, pages, chapters, whole books and the like). This is how we get sense from language: in sequences or groups of words. But we also get sense from context: who's saying what to whom? What are the phrases around the phrase that I'm actually reading? What happened in the poem, play or story that came before the bit I'm hearing or reading? How do plots 'unfold'? How do we 'get' character? How do flashbacks and flash forwards work? How do I know who is speaking in a story? How do I get it that some writing is about what's going in people's minds and some of it isn't? And so on.

These are things that we have to learn if we are to understand writing.

One of the great things about poems is that the sequences are often very memorable. This may be because they have a regular rhythm, a regular rhyme, a regular shape, sequences that have something that 'chimes' – e.g. alliteration, assonance, some other kind of 'echoing' effect, repetition of words, or phrases; symmetrical balancing of words or phrases and so on.

All this means that poems are great ways of learning how language is much more than words, but that it comes to us in groups.

So, poems are a great way of learning that language is more than words: it's about sequences of words.

4. Flowing from all the previous points is one about dialect and 'register'. One of the problems for children reading for understanding of the written code is that writing is not speech. In other words, having spent five years learning how to speak and understand speech (and all its specific ways of going on), children have to not only learn how to lift signs off the page so that they correspond to words, they also have to unpack the particular methods that writing uses which are different from speech. These are things like: writing usually gets to the end of a train of thought without self-interrupting, without being interrupted by someone else, without repetition, without lots of hesitation, without lots of 'ums' and 'ers', without phrases like 'you know what I mean?' 'eh?'

Writing can have a train of thought (usually a sentence) that has more subordinate clauses in it, than we usually say when we're talking. The most common of these is the relative using 'who', 'which', 'that' and sometimes 'where'. Instead: oten in speech we start a new bit beginning with an 'It', 'This' or 'That'. Quite often in writing we put subordinate clauses beginning with words like 'When', 'Because', 'Although' (and many others) in front of the main clause, when in speech we tend to put them after. (None of this is a rule, these are just tendencies).

If, as I've said, poetry is a bridge between the oral and the written but it is itself a written form, then in a way it's a method of cheating the reader to get hold of written structures through the ear, ie orally. This is great for children to get the sound of written sequences of language. They will probably remember whole chunks of written language. It's as if they've been tricked into getting the way writing works into their heads.

So, reading poetry together is a great way to learn how writing works.

5. One of the tasks facing us in education is how to help children get hold of abstract thought, abstract ideas. A good deal of poetry appears to be just the opposite (by no means all of it, though). A lot of poetry is about feelings, looking closely at specific objects, processes, scenes and people. Some of it is focussed on telling a story. Some of it is focussed on the sensation of actions and processes. Some of it is about celebrating or talking about cultural features of our lives: how we eat, sing, have ceremonies, how we dress. Some of it is about the kinds of dialogues we have with others. None of this seems to be about abstract thought.

But . . .

. . . if we invite children to talk about poems, they will inevitably select aspects of poems they enjoy or are puzzled by and the like. Sometimes this takes them very quickly into telling or describing something analogous. It may take them into telling an analogous story or anecdote. In its own way this is doing something abstract. It involves selecting one item from many from the poem, and selecting from many memories, a memory that overlaps with the one in the poem. This is in effect doing what we invite children to do when they make a 'series' out of objects in maths. It is a matter of creating a category to hold a thought from the poem and a thought in their head. Some have called these 'schemas'. So, in what may seem like quite inconsequential comments and stories, may well be something sophisticated going on: the bringing to the surface and/or the creation of schema. These may involve feelings, processes, actions, sights, scenes and much else besides.

So, poems are a great way to help children make the transition from thinking in concrete, specific ways towards making abstractions. Or, in brief, talking about poems is a great way to help children with abstract thought.

6. It's very hard to remember how we thought of language when we were young. I have a feeling that quite a few children think that the stuff they say every day in not part of the same thing that goes on with reading and writing in school. Though we talk of the 'English language', in fact we create compartments for different kinds of usage. If I was a child again, I think it would be very easy for me to think that the specialised use of language that goes on in school, was not really 'mine'. It's something that was owned by teachers, text books, dictionaries and exams and the like. I think that one of our tasks in schools is to help children get a sense that this 'school language' can be taken over and owned by children. The great advantage of reading, hearing, performing and talking about poems, is that a good deal of them are easy to own. Parts or all of them can, with repetition, become very easy to learn off by heart. This is one way for school language to become owned by children.

So, poetry reading is a great way for children to make formal language their own.

7. Related to this is the fact that poetry in the twentieth century not only copied and adapted itself – e.g. limericks, sonnets, ballads, and the like, but started to copy and adapt any form of language that was out there. It could do this by e.g. parodying prayers, or imitating ads, mimicking the way politicians, or scientists, or teachers or anyone spoke; it could imitate street signs, street cries and much else. I often think that poetry is a 'scavenger'. Unlike almost any other use of language, poetry feels free to grab an example of a type of language-use from anywhere and play with it.

Schools usually ask children to do something very different with language. We ask children to perform tasks to fit an already-made shape and purpose: recounts, stories with beginnings, middles and ends; sentences that contain certain fixed characteristics like fronted adverbials or relative clauses. The great thing about poetry is that it can home in on any way of speaking or writing it likes and do what it wants with it. Think of the poems in Allan Ahlberg's 'Please Mrs Butler'. A lot of them are in a 'teacher's voice'. Children hearing or reading these can get very quickly that poems can borrow anyone's way of talking. It isn't a fixed 'genre'. You can just decide to adopt a voice and run with it.

This suggests that it's OK to treat language as something to grab, or plunder or play with. This helps children feel (as above) that language can be theirs. They can own it.

So, poetry can help children see that language is theirs to adopt and adapt.

8. One of the key concepts that we want to help children get hold of is 'empathy'. One way to look at empathy is to say that it is about understanding how others think and feel. Because poetry is often about a poet's thoughts and feelings, if we enjoy a poem, there is every chance that we are developing our empathy.

There is another way to think of empathy: it is about getting to see how other people's culture(s) work. Poems are good for this too. A lot of poems (some would argue it's 'all poems' but let's leave that to one side for the moment!) express people's culture. Whether it's talking about food, home, school, hopes, fears, habits, particular ways of talking, slangs, celebrations, styles of dress, proverbs, sayings and much more, poems often show us culture. If it's done in a catchy, interesting, funny, intriguing, even sad way, we might be caught up in thinking about people who have cultures different from our own. This is another way of thinking about empathy.

Either way, poems are great ways to help us learn empathy.

9. Related to this, poems are often about values. The poet is quite often trying to say that such-and-such is important or valuable or worthwhile. It may not be the 'thing' at the heart of the poem but the fact that the poet is looking at the 'thing', dwelling on it, or wondering about it, spending time gazing at it or trying to understand it. It may be because there is a story at the heart of the poem which indicates that one or more things are worthwhile, or significant.

Ultimately, education will involve values, even if it's not more than saying that 'this subject is worth studying' or 'it is worthwhile for you to learn this, learn about that' or just that it's worthwhile learning, per se.

So, poems are a great way to engage with values.

10. Schools spend some time in a month engaging with children's feelings. Some people do 'circle time', others do it through specific lessons. Some do it when 'issues' crop up, e.g. bullying, bereavement, loneliness and the like. Some work to a syllabus.

Clearly, a good deal of poetry talks about feelings. They often show someone or some people experiencing something and implying or talking about emotions.

This means that poems are a great way to bring emotions to the surface. There is an advantage in that because a poem will be about the emotions of the person/people in the poem, the reader doesn't have to talk about their own individual experience (which may be too raw, or too embarrassing to talk about directly) in order to engage with the feeling that is bothering them. The reader or listener can talk about the feelings of the person/people in the poem instead. Poems can deflect or 'contain' the emotions of the reader/listener so that they are 'safe' even as they engage with those emotions.

So, poems can be safe ways to engage with feelings in a helpful way.

11. Some schools do philosophy to help children think about how we think. We have different strategies for thinking about things. Across a range of poems, we come face to face with poets using different ways of thinking about things: sometimes very empirically as if they're being scientists, sometimes very speculatively as if they are 'brainstorming', sometimes relating personal experience to shared experience, sometimes in very open-ended ways, sometimes in very closed-ended ways and so on.

This means that poems are one way we can begin a discussion about how we think and how we have different ways of thinking. We can discuss how we let emotions affect our judgement. We can discuss how sometimes we say one thing and mean another and much more. Poems often explore these areas.

Because to engage with this requires 'interpretation', poems are a) great places to start discussions about how we think but also b) a great way to discover that we are all 'interpreters', young or old, capable of coming up with ways of making a meaning out of some words or all the words in a poem.

I hope these 11 points will help you justify the activity of reading, sharing, performing and talking about poems. Please note, I'm not talking here about any specific or targeted activities other than just these. In some future parts of this 'Poetry in the Primary School' I will tackle some more targeted activities. However, I don't want to suggest that 'targeted' is necessarily any better than the kinds of sharing I suggested in Poetry in the Primary School 1.Please remember that poets write poems in order that people who read them have conversations: with themselves as individuals and with others. By reading, sharing, performing and talking about poems, you will be going with the flow of the art form of poetry. You are being true to poetry. That's worth something too, of course!

Part 3: How to Look at a Poem Closely

I'm imagining sats-free sessions in primary schools, where you can read, talk about and discover poetry without worrying too much about the exact questions that SATs ask.

There are ways of doing close reading of poems which don't impose on the reading precise formulas. As you know these often go along the lines of proving that this or that poetic device ('alliteration' and the like) is 'effective' before anyone's had a chance of deciding that it is! Another formula is the one where the child has to guess what was in the poet's head and state that as a reason why this or that poetic device is there: 'the poet introduced alliteration because it gives a sense of murmuring secrets' or some such. Again, no one knows this to be the case and anyway for another reader the alliteration in question may give another 'sense' altogether.

Leaving that to one side, are there ways in which primary age children can do some close reading of poems, which really explore how poems work without some of these more daft ways of closing down interpretation? I think there are. A more theoretical framework for this is in the section I did of a 'matrix of responses'.

1. You vary the class teaching from working in pairs, on their own and in whole class situations. For the close reading to work, groups larger than two will probably not work so well.

2. The first question you ask the children in pairs to talk about is whether there is anything in the poem, or the poem as a whole 'reminds them of anything that has happened to them, or anything that has happened to someone they know'. You can model an answer for this question as a way of kicking things off, of course. Get them to talk in pairs for a couple of minutes and share some of these in the whole class. Then ask them to explain to each other 'why' and 'how' they are reminded. Model this too. Then share some of these in a whole class.

This enables the children to see that poems are not only about what they appear to be about (!) but that we as readers are 'in' poems too. Our experiences are part of the way in which we are able to interpret the poem.

3. Second question is to follow the same pattern but invite the children to think about other poems, stories, plays, TV programmes, computer games – ie any other 'text' – and see if there is anything in the poem or the poem as a whole that reminds them of a 'text' they know. Model this. Get them to talk in pairs. Share some of the responses. Then ask 'why' and 'how'. Model this, then share some of them.

4. The third area to get into is the children's own questions. Ask them in pairs to come up with questions about the poem as a whole: any part of the poem; questions for the poet; questions for anyone or any thing in the poem.

Break these down one by one, modelling some questions yourself, getting them to talk in pairs and sharing in the class. When you hear the questions, write them up where they can see them.

By the end of a few minutes you should have a good few questions.

Talk with the whole class about which questions look interesting and puzzling enough to try and answer. Get them to talk in pairs to try to answer these questions, then share with the whole class. Get them also to discuss how to find out answers to questions that you can't solve. Internet? Books? Someone they know? Someone you know?

You could talk about going to college and how you found out answers to questions about poems, books and stories.

5. Take stock of where you've got to with the poem. What do we know, what don't we know, what would we like to know? At this point you could introduce terminology where you thought it was relevant and helpful. Or you could hold that back for the next part of the 'looking closely'.

6. I've called this 'secret strings'. All poems hang together and express what they want to express by unstated or 'secret' means. So a poem that rhymes doesn't say 'I'm rhyming'! It just does it. Same goes for its beat, metre, or any of the sounds it uses like alliteration, assonance, repetition, 'framing', patterning into verses, rhyme schemes etc. None of it is 'announced'. Same again for the patterns of images a poem uses e.g. around a theme like 'light' or a specific colour, or a words about sadness. Same yet again for contrasts and opposites. Poems often move forwards by contrasting images or moods or scenes. These too are patterns which come 'unannounced'. But these secret strings are part of how a poem has a meaning. So, if I write: 'rain raining, rain raining, rain raining', I'm not only saying 'It's raining'. I'm also saying, 'it's raining a lot and it's going on and on.' I do that without telling it! When we look at 'secret strings' we discover how some of these poetic ways of affecting us are done.

So you say to the children that they are 'poem detectives' and it's their job to find the 'secret strings'. You can model some of these: ones that are to do with sound (like rhyme, rhythm, alliteration and assonance); some to do with imagery that are 'same' and some that are to do with opposite or contrast. Then put them in pairs, with a copy of the poem in front of them, and they can draw the string in a colour on the poem.

The rule is: if you can justify why a string is a string, it is a string. You can say that quite often the poets don't know their own strings. If they don't believe you, you can tell them that I've said it!

So, now in pairs they hunt for strings, and then you can invite them to share these.

You can take this one step further and invite them to come up with possible reasons why the poet made these strings, whether they poet knew it or not.

7. After you have done these 6 stages of looking at a poem, I promise you, you will have explored many, many aspects of the poem. Some will be the same as the kinds of things that you think are important about the poem and some not. It may well change the way you think about aspects of the poem. If you are concerned that the class haven't got hold of what you think is the most important aspect of the poem, you are now in a good position to offer that to them as your view. They, meanwhile, are in a good position to examine what you say and offer their thoughts on the matter.

Part 4: Children Responding to Poems

This is a 'matrix' for use by teachers or anyone else wanting to do just this: analyse the kinds of talk and writing that pupils do in response to literature. It's not intended to be a strict, fixed matrix; some of the categories overlap. Not all of the categories fit all situations. It's intended to be both a work in progress and part of a process in which teachers and researchers adapt and refine what I've written as part of developing their own ideas in practice.

The Matrix

When we make comments about literature (or when children or school students are in pairs or groups in a classroom) it's possible to evaluate those comments, notes or passages of writing.

One way to do this is to make transcripts of what they are saying.

These can be when they are in conversation with the teacher or with each other in pairs or groups.

The nature of the conversation will depend greatly on how it is set up: what kinds of questions the teachers set, or indeed if the questions originate from the students themselves.

This is worth experimenting with along the lines of what seems to be the most useful and fruitful way to set things up so that pupils do the most amount of engaged reflection.

When you look at a transcript of how the students talk, it's possible to categorise the comments. Here are some suggested categories:

1. Experiential – this where we relate what is in the text with something that has happened to me or to someone I know. One useful trigger question for this is simply: 'Is there anything you've just read which reminds you of something that has happened to you, or someone you know? – Why?- How?'

2. Intertextual – this is where we relate what is in the text to another text. One useful trigger for this question is: 'Is there anything you've just read which reminds you of something you've read, seen on TV, online, at the cinema, a song, a play, a show? – Why? How?'

3. Intratextual – this is where we relate one part of the text to another part. One useful trigger for this question arises out of a moment in a piece of literature where we ask: 'But how do we know that, using something or anything that came before?' (I have a nickname for this which younger children enjoy: I call it 'harvesting' – that is, collecting up information or feelings from other parts of the text.

4. Interrogative – where we ask questions of the text and voice puzzles and are tentative about something. One trigger question for this is, 'Is there anything here we don't understand or are puzzled by?' This can be followed up by, 'Is there anyone here who thinks they can answer that?' And 'Does anyone have any ideas about how we can go about finding an answer to that?'

5. Semantic – where we make comments about what something in the text means.

6. Structural – where we indicate we are making a comment about how a part or whole of the piece has been put together, 'constructed'. (One way we do this is by making comparisons across from one text to another noticing 'how' different authors do things.)

7. Selective analogising – where we make an analogy between one part of the text and something from anywhere else (e.g. as in 1, 2, 3). There will be an implied 'set' or 'series' being constructed here around a motif or theme or feeling. This process of analogising is extremely important even though it is often masked by seemingly trivial comments like, 'I remember a time when I was sad . . . ' The importance lies in the fact that the pupil at this point is in fact creating an unstated abstraction. It is halfway (or more) towards abstract thought. Perhaps, it becomes fully abstract when the pupil(s) give that 'set' a name: eg 'Sadness' or 'Emotions' or some such.

8. Speculative – where we make speculations about what might happen, what could have happened. This is any kind of comment in the category of 'I wonder . . . ' or 'What if . . . '

9. Reflective – where we make interpretative statements often headed by 'I think . . . ' ie more committed than 'speculative'.

10. Narratological – where we make comments about how the story has been told e.g. about narrators, methods of unfolding a story, what is held back, what is revealed. ('Narratology'). It may include an awareness of how stories have episodes, and sudden 'turns' or 'red herrings', flashbacks, flash forwards etc. Why dialogue is used, why e.g. indirect speech is used, why or how interior monologues are used. It can also be about why or how individual words, phrases, clauses, sentences and expressions are used. It might also look at narrative methods like e.g. looking at story openings and techniques, or how to create tension, how to create awe, horror, surprise and so on. This will overlap with 'effects'.

11. Evaluative – where we make value judgements about aspects of a text of the whole. These can be comments about significance, 'what the author is getting at . . . ', or 'why someone in the text said 'x''.

12. Eureka moments – where we announce that we have suddenly 'got it'.

13. Effects – where we sense that an 'effect' has been created in us (or in others we have observed) because of the way something has been written. 'This made me jump..' 'This made me sad . . . ' Response journals, or post-it notes on poem-posters and the like can 'grab' these very well. This can be at several levels: individual choice of words, expressions; how a paragraph or chapter develops; how characters interact; the outcome of events . . . etc.

14. Storying – this is where we make a comment which is in essence another story. This is not trivial. As with 'analogising' (above) will almost certainly involve the making of a 'set' or a 'series' ie something has been selected from the original text in order to trigger off the new one. This is an implied generalisation. The academic Carol Fox points out that for very young children, storying has to carry a good deal of intellectual thought to do with e.g. understanding how the material world works ('cognition' of e.g. numbers, shape, scientific principles), how and why people think in certain ways ('philosophy', 'morality'), understanding and interpreting emotions (often reading this off expressions on people's faces in illustrations) and more.

15. Descriptive, – where we recount aspects of the text. This may well be more significant than it first appears because we can ask, why was this moment selected for the recount? Again, this may well be part of 'analogising' and/or 'storying'.

16. Grammatical – where we draw attention to the structure of sentences – syntax, or how individual words are used grammatically.

17. Prosodic – where we draw attention to the sound of parts of the whole of a piece ie the 'music' of it. I have outlined in my book *What is Poetry?* (Walker) how you can invite pupils to determine this themselves by using what I call 'secret strings' ie finding links between parts of poems whether linked by sound or by meaning.

18. Effect of interactions: where we draw attention to how people interact ie how people (any character) treats another, how they 'relate' and what is the outcome of how they relate. In my experience, this is more valuable than simply trying to describe 'character'.

19. Imaginative – where we move to another artistic medium in order to interpret what we have been reading or viewing . . . this may well involve more 'generalising' or 'abstract thought' than first appears because it involves 'selecting' something from the original text and creating some kind of 'set' or 'series' with it in creating something new. If pupils are asked 'why' this can be teased out.

20. Emotional flow: these are comments which show how feelings towards the protagonists change. Some people have invented 'flow maps' where you can draw up a kind of graph or chart, with the key moments in the plot along the bottom axis, and emotional states on the vertical axis . . . then you can label the line on the graph.

21. 'Author intention' – this might come partly under the category of 'speculative' – above – ie what the author could have written. Or it might be part of 'effect' ie how has the author created an effect. Word of warning: if this is separated from 'how it affected me' or 'how it affected someone else', this is of course speculation. The routine of a good deal of 'criticism' is to assume precisely the opposite ie because there is a certain literary feature – e.g. alliteration using a 'hard' sound, that it has a specific 'effect' – e.g. being insistent or heavy – and that the author intended these, which may or may not be the case.

22. Contextual – every piece of literature comes from a time and place. The person reading or spectating it will not be in exactly the same time and place. Many responses and critical ideas and thoughts go on because of this 'gap'. Students may well know or speculate about the gap, or the context ('They didn't used to do that sort of thing in those days') and of course, may ask questions and/or we offer them information or they are encouraged to research the context(s).

23. Representational or symbolic – where we make comments about what we think something 'represents'. This might be about 'character' where we say that a person 'represents' the class or type he or she comes from . . . 'typical x kind of person'. It might be about parts of the landscape or the nature of the landscape – as it represents a particular kind of challenge to the protagonist. It could be a feature in the landscape/cityscape ie a particular kind of tree or building. It could be a single object that represents something more than itself – a torn piece of paper. And so on.

24. Extra-textual – comments that have apparently nothing to do with what's in the text and are about what's going on in the classroom or they are about pupils' interactions. Often these are as they seem to be but just occasionally they may well relate to how the pupils are interpreting e.g. a personal comment about 'You always say things like that . . . ' may well be an indirect comment about this text and others.

25. Causation – it's been pointed out to me that I've overlooked the response where the reader/listener talks about people's motives or reactions or feelings as a result or consequence of something that happened earlier. The key words here that the reader/listener uses are of course things like 'because' /'that's why he/she . . . '/'so he/she . . . ' When young readers/listeners do this, it may well be significant because he/she will be grappling with the logic, chronology of the text, or of characters' behaviour. (The word the national curriculum uses here is 'inference'.)

Note: In terms of teaching, we may want to emphasise one, some or several of these responses. We may want to develop one, some or several. We may want to induce the students to ask 'why' about any or all of them so that we can advance their ability to reason and rationalise. We may want to compare any of these with how the teacher or critics have responded in order to take the comments and thinking to a new level.

Part 5: Trigger Questions

Based on Michael Rosen's 'matrix' of the types of comments which children make about texts (2017), from which the wording of the descriptions is mostly borrowed. See http://michaelrosenblog.blogspot.co.uk

While reading, children will make comments spontaneously, or within a range of organised contexts – free discussion, free or journal writing, structured talk in pairs, small groups or as a class, talk or writing in role, drama and so on.

However, often comments are in response to questions, sometimes posed by a teacher or other adult but sometimes posed by other pupils. Below are some typical trigger question stems. Of course, it is often the subsequent follow-up questions ('WHY?') which prompt the deepest and most interesting thinking.

Experiential	Is there anything you've just read which reminds you of something that has happened to you, or someone you know? Why? How?
Where we relate what is in the text with something that has happened to me or to someone I know.	Have you ever . . . ? Does that remind you of a time when you . . . ?
Has anyone ever . . . ?	Does anyone you know . . . ? Have you ever seen . . . ?

Experiential (continued)	Has anything like that ever happened . . . ? When are you most like . . . ? When do you feel like . . . ? Which character are you most . . . ? Do you recognise . . . ?
Intertextual Where we relate what is in the text to another text.	Is there anything you've just read which reminds you of something you've read/ seen on TV or online or at the cinema/a song/a play/a show..? Why? How? Where else have you seen . . . ? Have you read any other . . . ? Does this remind you of any . . . ? Is this like a . . . ? Is this typical of . . . ? How is this different from . . . ?
Intratextual Might that bit . . . ? Where we relate one part of the text to another part.	But how do we know that . . . ? Does that remind you of any . . . ? Are there any other examples of . . . ? Is there a pattern . . . ? Does that echo any . . . ? How is this different from . . . ? What's changed in . . . ? Were there any clues to . . . ?

Interrogative	Is there anything here we don't understand or are puzzled by?
Where we ask questions of the text and voice puzzles and are tentative about something.	Any questions about . . . ? What would you ask the . . . ? What don't we know about . . . ? What do we need to know, in order to . . . ? Is anything missing from? Is there something that we haven't . . . ?
Semantic I wonder what . . . ? Where we make comments about what something in the text means.	What might that mean? What do you think the writer is saying, when they . . . ? Does this tell us anything about . . . ? What does that imply/suggest/ indicate about . . . ? Is it clear what . . . ? Can we be sure what . . . ? Where does the text say..?
Structural Where we indicate we are making a comment about how a part or whole of the piece has been put together, 'constructed'.	How does the start/middle/ ending . . . ? Is there a pattern in . . . ? Is there a shape to . . . ? What do we . . . first? Next, how do we . . . ? Does that remind you of any . . . ? Does this echo any . . . ? What changes, as . . . ? How has the writer built . . . ? Is there a repeated . . . ?

Speculative What might . . . ? Where we make speculations about what might happen, what could have happened.	What could . . . ? Might . . . ? What might . . . if . . . ? What do you guess could . . . ? What could have led to . . . ? What might have . . . ? Any theories about . . . ? Why do you suppose . . . ?
Reflective Where we make interpretative statements often headed by 'I think . . . '	What's your impression of . . . ? What, to you, is . . . like? What do you think happened when . . . ? Why do you think . . . ? What will . . . ? How do you suppose . . . ? Do you think . . . ?
Narratological Where we make comments about how the story has been told, e.g. about narrators, methods of unfolding a story, what is held back, what is revealed. ('Narratology'). It may include an awareness of how stories have episodes, and sudden 'turns' or 'red herrings', flashbacks, flash forwards etc.	What has the writer done to . . . ? Do you think we are meant to notice . . . ? What isn't the writer . . . ? Who is telling . . . ? Whose view is . . . ? How have we been . . . ? How has the writer built . . . ? What happened to the story there?

Evaluative	What do you think the writer is getting at . . . ?
Where we make value judgements about aspects of a text of the whole. These can be comments about significance, 'what the author is getting at . . . ', or 'why someone in the text said 'x''.	Why do you think the characters said . . . ? When does the writer show most clearly . . . ? What, overall, is the effect of . . . ? What is your favourite . . . ? What is the most effective . . . ? How well does . . . ? What is the most . . . ? Is there anything you didn't think . . . ?
Ah! Eureka moment Where we announce that we have suddenly 'got it'.	Anyone got a new idea about . . . ? Any comments on what just . . . ? Any breakthroughs?
Effects Where we sense that an 'effect' has been created in us (or in others we have observed) because of the way something has been written.	How did you feel when . . . ? How might that make . . . ? What feeling does . . . ? What's the effect of . . . ? Which bit make you feel . . . ? Which part might create . . . ? Can you describe how you felt when . . . ? What's your own reaction to . . . ?

Storying This is where we make a comment which is in essence another story, triggered by something in the text being read.	What do people usually do when . . . ? Do you know any . . . ? Anyone had their own . . . ? When have you . . . ? Does that remind you of any . . . ? Has anyone had a . . . ? Anyone know a story about a . . . ?
Descriptive Where we recount aspects of the text. This may well be more significant than it first appears because we can ask why details were. Which part do you . . . ?	What do you remember about . . . ? What sticks most in your mind about . . . ? What moment do you remember most from . . . ? Can you remind us . . . ? How would you sum up . . . ? What happened when . . . ? How did we get to . . . ? What happened to make . . . ?
Grammatical Where we draw attention to the structure of sentences – syntax, or how individual words are used grammatically.	I wonder what makes that sentence . . . ? What do you notice about . . . ? In that sentence, how has the writer . . . ? Where has the writer . . . ? Which sentences are most . . . ? Which word makes the . . . ?

Prosodic Where we draw attention to the sound of parts of the whole of a piece – the 'music' of it. Let's try . . .	Let's listen to how . . . If you say that aloud, how . . . ? Where does it sound most . . . ? Listen to that but. How . . . ? How do the sounds of . . . ? Is there anything about how the words sound that . . . ?
Effect of Interactions Can we work out . . . ? Where we draw attention to how people interact with or treat one another, how they 'relate' and what is the outcome of how they relate – often more valuable than simply trying to describe 'character'.	How does . . . treat . . . ? Why do you think she . . . ? How did . . . talk to . . . ? What do they seem to think about each other? Which characters seem to . . . ? Can we work out how . . . feels about . . . ? Why do you think . . . tells . . . ? How do . . . and . . . feel when . . . ? What do you notice about . . . and . . . ?
Imaginative Where we move to another artistic medium in order to interpret what we have been reading or viewing.	How could we show this by . . . ? What would that look like if . . . ? What would . . . say if . . . ? How might . . . describe . . . ? Can you imagine what . . . ? What would an actor playing . . . ?

Emotional Flow	How have your feelings about . . . changed?
These are comments which show how feelings towards the protagonists change.	How did you used to feel about . . . ?
	Does . . . still make you think . . . ?
Any thoughts about . . . ?	Is that the same as when . . . ?
	What's different now about . . . ?
	Any thoughts about how . . . is different . . . ?
	How do you feel now about . . . ?
	When did you feel most . . . about . . . ?
	At what point did you start to feel . . . ?
'Author Intention'	What do you think is likely to . . . ?
This might come partly under the category of 'speculative' – what the author could have written. Or it might be part of 'effect – how the author has created an effect (possiblyintentionally.)	How do you think we are meant to . . . ?
	Do you think the writer has a plan for . . . ?
	How might we be supposed to react when . . . ?
	What do you think the writer wants us to . . . ?
What do you suspect . . . ?	What do you suspect the writer is doing when . . . ?
	What might that word be meant to . . . ?

Contextual	How do you think we might read this differently from . . . ?
Every piece of literature comes from a time and place. The person reading or spectating will not be in exactly the same time and place. Many responses and critical ideas and thoughts go on because of this 'gap'.	When this was written, what/ how/who might . . . ? What can we guess about where/when this is taking place? What do we need to know about . . . in order to understand . . . ? Is there anything we know now which . . . ?
Pupils may well know or speculate about the gap, or the context ('They didn't used to do that sort of thing in those days') and of course, may ask questions and/or we offer them information or they are encouraged to research the context(s).	Why do you think they felt/ thought/ believed . . . ?
Representational or Symbolic	How do you think that might be important? What kind of. . . is . . . ?
Where we make comments about what we think something 'represents'. This might be about 'character' where we say that a person 'represents' the class or type he or she comes from . . . 'typical x kind of person'.	Are they typical of any . . . ? Could it stand for a . . . ? What does that mean for . . . ? Does that make us think of any . . . ? Does anything symbolise . . . ?

Representational or Symbolic (continued) It might be about parts of the landscape or the nature of the landscape – as it represents a particular kind of challenge to the protagonist. It could be a feature in the landscape/cityscape i.e. a particular kind of tree or building. It could be a single object that represents something more than itself – a torn piece of paper. And so on.	Might it represent something else? What represents . . . ? Could it be symbolic of something else?

These trigger questions come from James Durran of NATE and are based on my matrix in Part 4.

Part 6: Writing

I. I've written two books on how to help children write poems: *Did I Hear You Write?* published first by Andre Deutsch and then by Five Leaves Press. You can find it in libraries or second-hand online.

The second one is much more recent and is published by Walker Books. It's called *What is Poetry? An Essential Guide for Reading and Writing Poems*. It is available to order through any bookshop, it's in libraries and you can find it online.

In this book I talk about some classic poems and how they're put together and how I respond to them. I talk about some poems that I've written and how I came to write them and what methods I used to write them. I also have a set of activities for children reading the book.

I won't summarise what I've written in these two books here.

2. If you follow some of the processes I've described in the 5 previous chapters, I promise you that part of the problem of getting children to write poems will already be solved for you. That's to say, primary school children will start to say to you and the class that they want to write poems. This is because poetry is 'infectious'. Poems are, as I've said, constructed with 'hooks', methods and meanings that are designed to stick in readers' and listeners' minds. If you share lots of poems, talk about them and explore them in enjoyable ways, children will want to have a go themselves. They will also have in their heads many models for how poems work. If say, you are doing the 'poetry concert' thing alongside a 'poem a week on the wall' and they all have notebooks where they put poems they like, then their heads are full of parts of poems and even whole poems. This gives them and you a 'repertoire' or 'gallery' of poems to refer to.

3. Building on this idea, the simplest and easiest way to trigger the writing of a poem is to say to the children something along the lines of 'We could write a poem like that!'.

That simple sentence hides something a bit more complex. When we say, 'like that' it can mean – a poem that sounds something like that; a poem that is shapes something like that; a poem that has a meaning like that; a poem that picks up from the poem a single image and runs with that.

You can model these different ways of what you mean when you say, 'We could write a poem like that.'

4. Once children start writing poems in a class, one key thing is to get them 'distributed'. By this, I mean getting them up on walls, into say, blogs which can be seen by any audience you choose – the class, the school, or whatever, into booklets, into your own school-made anthologies, performed in shows for the class, for the school, for a show with parents.

5. The moment you start sharing poems, one key thing is to allow time for you and the children to say what aspects of the poems they and you read or hear that you or they would like to have a go at yourselves. This is the positivity response that helps you build together a reading-writing community.

You might also want to integrate comments about the poems you've read (by established poets) and the poems that the children and you (?) are writing. So you can ask the children to spend time sometimes talking about 'echoes'. What 'echoes' can you hear in the poem by a child that echo back to a poem they've heard? You have to make sure that this isn't an accusation! No one is saying that to write a poem that is a bit like another poem is 'stealing'. Poets through time have always been in conversation with other poets through the poems they write. They echo, imitate, parody and 'scavenge' from other poems. That's fine. It's a great way to understand and interpret poems if you explore these similarities, overlaps and echoes.

6. Are there specific techniques to write poems? Well, yes and no. Yes – clearly, you can decide, 'Today I'm going to write a limerick. A limerick has a specific rhyme scheme. I'm going to write one just like that.' That's fine. There are books full of how to start writing a poem in this way: starting with a particular poetic form. When I do poetry workshops in schools, these are usually one-offs. I arrive, do a workshop and go away. Given that that is the time and space available, I will adopt a way of running a workshop that is partly along these lines. I show the children a poem I wrote that has a chorus. I invite them to write a poem with me collectively that uses the same chorus. I use 'trigger questions' to pick up on the themes of 'what can you see?', 'what can you hear?' 'What are people saying?' 'What are you saying?' 'What are you imagining?' and slot the answers to these within the chorus.

Then I suggest that they can opt to do one of these on their own, in pairs. They could change the chorus, change the questions, change the order of the questions. They could experiment with taking out the chorus once they had written the poem. Or use the chorus as a 'frame' rather than a chorus. Or, – and I always ways this – they could write in any way they like, taking off from anything they've heard so far. As the poem I start with is often my 'After Dark' poem, this quite often triggers poems that are completely different from the structure that I set out with.

7. Another workshop that I do, involves me reading one of my poems that has a mystery at the heart of it. There is something that has gone on 'off-stage' that isn't mentioned in the poem. I invite the children to write about that moment. In a sense nearly all stories have these off-stage moments, as well as others which either come before or after the poem, story or play. A great way to get children to write is to find these off-stage moments and write about them or write them as part of how a character or a thing is 'thinking' in these offstage moments. I have a nickname-phrase for these moments as 'What did Goldilocks say when she got home?' Think of, for example, what did Hansel or Gretel or the trees in the forest, think when Hansel and Gretel realised that they had been abandoned and the birds had eaten the bread that Hansel dropped?

8. A further workshop I do involves getting the children to think metaphorically without telling them! I invite the children to think about riddles. We share some. We tell them to each other.

I say that today we're going to write some things that are a bit like riddles. I invite them to choose an object, or a process or a concept (like 'time' say). Then I invite them to say what that object can 'see', what it can 'hear', what it 'imagines', what is it 'afraid of', what it 'hopes for', what it 'dreams of'? (There's no limit to these, you can think of as many or as different as you like.)

Then we discuss how riddles often have at their heart a 'paradox'. 'I stay on the corner but I go round the world. What am I? A postage stamp.' We discuss paradox and think of other riddle paradoxes, e.g. a chair has legs but can't walk. A clock has a face but can't smile etc.

So can they put a paradox amongst the answers or after the answers to the questions they asked?

Then they read the riddles out loud and the class has to guess what the object is.

The follow-up to this is to discuss metaphor and 'figurative' language. By animating an object or a process or a concept, they have made a metaphor and explored it. Remind them of how they can use this as a way of writing other poems. When reading poems, you can discuss how poets are often using this 'riddling' method of inviting us to think about how objects, processes and concepts work.

9. I won't go on with this as I have a few more in the two books I mentioned at the beginning and as I've said, you'll find many, many more in the books available in libraries and bookshops. I'll finish by saying that no matter how immediately effective these 'triggers' are, at the end of the day, 'trust the poem, trust the child'. That's to say, keep reading and talking about and performing poems – whether these are by established poets, you, the children. By encouraging positivity in how to talk about each other's poems you foster the urge to write, and the urge to experiment and improve. By encouraging the children to talk about poems you encourage them to listen out for ways of writing and performing that excite and interest them. Your input can be decisive because you can introduce poems that they wouldn't otherwise come across.

Make yourself a finder-out of poems for the class. Tell the children when you've discovered a poem. Tell them that you're excited when they discover a poem you didn't know. Encourage them to do that: be poem explorers!

Most of these ideas and many more are in *What is Poetry? An Essential Guide to Reading and Writing Poetry* published by Walker Books. In that book, I have a section on some poems I've written and how I came to write them.

I often post thoughts on education, literature, and current affairs on my blog at: http://michaelrosenblog.blogspot.co.uk/

You can also follow my work at: http://www.michaelrosen.co.uk/